Lamb of God

BIBLE STUDY ABOUT JESUS & SCRIPTURE WRITING JOURNAL
~for Christian Women~

JoDitt
DESIGNS

5 WEEK BIBLE READING PLAN & PRAYER JOURNAL NOTEBOOK
+ BONUS SCRIPTURE COLORING BOOK PAGES
for Adults and Teen Girls

JoDitt Williams

Scripture quotations are from:

ESV® Bible (The Holy Bible, English Standard Version®), copyright © 2001 by Crossway, a publishing ministry of Good News Publishers. Used by permission. All rights reserved.

KING JAMES VERSION, (KJV) public domain.

Cover and Interior Design By JoDitt Williams

Lamb of God Bible Study About Jesus & Scripture Writing Journal for Christian Women: 5 Week Bible Reading Plan & Prayer Journal Notebook + Bonus Scripture Coloring Book Pages for Adults and Teen Girls

Copyright © 2021 JoDitt Williams | JoDitt Designs
Brighten the Corner Publishing
Stephenville, TX
Available from Amazon.com and other retail outlets

If you are interested in licensing these or any of JoDitt's artwork and designs, please email jdw@joditt.com

JoDitt Designs
Stephenville, TX 76401
www.joditt.com

ISBN: 978-0-9983846-1-0

This Journal
BELONGS TO:

_____

WHY SCRIPTURE WRITING?

Psalms 1 says that "blessed" is the person whose delight is in God's Word. Writing out Scripture is such a simple, easy way to *"delight"* in the Word of God.

Anyone one can do SCRIPTURE WRITING. It only takes a few minutes, and no perfection, skill or talent is needed.

"Thy word have I hid in mine heart, that I might not sin against thee." - Psalm 119:11

It has been proven that the simple act of writing something down helps you remember it (or hide it in your heart.)

Plus, I find that when I write out a Scripture, I often notice words, phrases or punctuation that I never even noticed before, even if I have read that exact verse a dozen times. And it can give that verse a whole new meaning to me.

If you are a visual or kinesthetic learner, like myself, you are going to love Scripture writing! There is just something about doing something with our hands, and seeing it with our eyes, that helps things to "click" in our brains.

I created this Scripture Writing Journal for you to make it super-simple. Just grab a pen or pencil, and you are good to go.

Personally, I like to use different colored pens or glitter gel pens, but any pen or pencil you have will work just fine.

- JoDitt

HOW TO USE THIS JOURNAL

The Reading/Writing plan is divided up into **5 weeks with 5 days per week**. There is one journal page per day, with an extra page at the end of each week for summary and/or highlights. *You may adapt to fit your schedule as needed.*

Each day, simply fill in the date, read the Bible verses, then write the selected Scripture using the lined journal area.

Write out the Scripture using your regular handwriting, paying close attention to each word. Capitalize, circle, (or highlight in some way) one or two words that stick out to you.

There should be plenty of space to write the suggested Scripture(s). In the room that is left, jot down any questions you have, things you observed, or "Aha" moments. If you want to dig deeper, you could look up the definition of a certain word or two, then copy the definition into your journal as well.

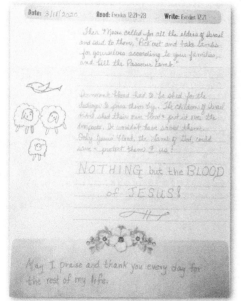

Alternately, you can write in LARGE letters to practice calligraphy or hand-lettering, allowing your letters to span 2-3 lines.

You can also write and/or doodle in the blank margins, or add stickers, etc.

Finally, there is a lovely box at the bottom of each page. Use this space to write out a prayer, or document the main thing you believe God is speaking to you through the Bible verses for that day.

On the weekly summary page, you can write out a summary of what you learned for the week, or jot down your highlights or biggest "take-away", or even write out a prayer conversation with God, writing out what you want to say to or ask God, and then also writing down what God is speaking to you.

BONUS PAGES

At the end of the journal are some bonus pages.

• **Clipart** - Copy this page onto copy paper or cardstock, then cut and paste the images into the margins of this journal or your Bible. You can also color the images if you like.

• **Word Art** - Copy onto copy paper and then trace the words onto the margins of this journal or onto the margins of your journaling Bible. Another option is to copy onto cardstock (or clear sticker paper) and stick onto journal cards, along with your own hand lettering to create your own Scripture memory cards.

• **Coloring Pages** - Color, then cut/tear out page, frame and hang in your home. Or use as tip-ins in your journaling Bible, or use as Scripture memory cards. You can also copy them onto copy paper or cardstock, and then color.

Get FREE Coloring & Creativity Tips & Tutorials, Scripture Printables & More at: joditt.com/lambofgodbonus

Learn more about delighting in the Word of God using color and creativity, on my blog at: joditt.com

Lamb of God

BIBLE READING & WRITING PLAN

DAY	READ	WRITE
❏ Day 1	Genesis 22:1-8	Genesis 22:8
❏ Day 2	Genesis 22:9-14	Genesis 22:13
❏ Day 3	Exodus 12:1-6	Exodus 12:3
❏ Day 4	Exodus 12:7-13	Exodus 12:11
❏ Day 5	Exodus 12:21-28	Exodus 12:21
❏ Day 6	Luke 22:7-13	Luke 22:7
❏ Day 7	1 Corinthians 5:6-8	1 Corinthians 5:7
❏ Day 8	John 1:29-34	John 1:29
❏ Day 9	Isaiah 53:1-9	Isaiah 53:7
❏ Day 10	Acts 8:26-35	Acts 8:32, 35
❏ Day 11	John 1:35-37	John 1:36
❏ Day 12	1 Peter 1:13-21	1 Peter 1:17-19
❏ Day 13	Revelation 5:1-6	Revelation 5:6
❏ Day 14	Revelation 5:7-10	Revelation 5:9-10
❏ Day 15	Revelation 5:11-14	Revelation 5:12
❏ Day 16	Revelation 7:9-12	Revelation 7:10
❏ Day 17	Revelation 7:13-17	Revelation 7:17
❏ Day 18	Revelation 12:7-12	Revelation 12:11
❏ Day 19	Revelation 19:6-10	Revelation 19:6b-8
❏ Day 20	Revelation 19:6-10	Revelation 19:9
❏ Day 21	Revelation 21:9-14	Revelation 21:9
❏ Day 22	Revelation 21:22-27	Revelation 21:22
❏ Day 23	Revelation 21:22-27	Revelation 21:23
❏ Day 24	Revelation 21:22-27	Revelation 21:27
❏ Day 25	Revelation 22:1-5	Revelation 22:3

Week 2 Highlights / Summary / Prayers

Week 3 Highlights / Summary / Prayers

Week 4 Highlights / Summary / Prayers

Week 5 Highlights / Summary / Prayers

Lamb of God Clipart

WORD ART

Copy onto copy paper and then trace onto the margins of this journal or your journaling Bible. Or copy onto cardstock (or clear sticker paper) and stick in the margins, or on journal cards, along with your own hand lettering to create your own Scripture memory cards.

Lamb of God

Lamb of God

LAMB OF GOD

Jesus

JESUS

Jesus

JESUS

Christ

CHRIST

Christ

CHRIST

Lamb of God

Lamb of God

LAMB OF GOD

PASSOVER

Passover

PASSOVER

Jesus

JESUS

Jesus

Christ

CHRIST

Christ

For Christ, our Passover lamb, has been sacrificed.

1 Corinthians 5:7

Behold, the LAMB of GOD, who takes away the sin of the world! —John 1:29

...YOU WERE RANSOMED...

WITH THE PRECIOUS

BLOOD OF CHRIST,

LIKE THAT OF A LAMB

WITHOUT BLEMISH OR SPOT.
- 1 PETER 1:18-19

And they OVERCAME him by the blood of the LAMB, & by the WORD of their testimony; and they LOVED not their LIVES unto the death.

Revelation 12:11

And the city has no need of **SUN** or **MOON** to **SHINE** on it, for the **GLORY** of God gives it **LIGHT**, and its **LAMP** is the Lamb.

– Revelation 21: 23

Then the **angel** showed me the river of the **water** of Life, bright as crystal, flowing from the **throne** of God <u>and</u> of the **Lamb**...

~ Revelation 22:1

NOTES

TEST PAGE

Use this page to test out colors, markers, etc.

ABOUT THE AUTHOR

JoDitt Williams is a passionate author, speaker, licensed artist, blogger and entrepreneur on a mission to brighten her little corner of the world and help others do the same.

Whether she is creating art using traditional methods or digitally, her style is always cute, colorful, cheerful and charming.

JoDitt has a passion for encouraging, uplifting and inspiring women to live a life full of joy, while gaining victory over fear. That's why she hosts a monthly Delight in the Word Challenge, and shares about hiding God's Word in your heart through color and creativity on her blog at:

---> **joditt.com**

JoDitt and her husband of over 30 years live in the great state of Texas, where they spend lots of time with their 2 married children and 3 grandchildren.

Join JoDitt's monthly Delight in the Word Challenges at:
joditt.com/ditwmchallenge/

Other Books by JoDitt:
(Available at joditt.com and on Amazon.com)

Delight in the Word of God Volume 1: Favorite Scriptures
- A Devotional Coloring Book & Journal for Adults & Teens

Self-Care Bible Study & Coloring Prayer Journal
- A 4 Week Guided Reading Plan Workbook for Women

SOAP Bible Study Journals & More

LEARN MORE AT JODITT.COM

Made in the USA
Monee, IL
13 July 2023

39208329R00037